# FROM FIRE AND FR(

## The Poetry Of
## FRANK S. FARELLO

ISBN:  9798284541456

# DEDICATION

To my Angel;

       my Love;

              my Best Friend;

                     my Wife;

                            my Pattie –

life would have no meaning without you!

# AND FOR...

My Children:  Frank; Evamarie; Sean
My Grandchildren:  Ryan; Emma; Sara; Brandyn; Adrianna; Mason
My Daughters-in-law:  Mary and Kristin
My Son-in-law:  Brian

# VERY SPECIAL THANKS TO:

Susan Romano

(A good friend whose advice and interest all those years ago is still so greatly appreciated.  Quadrinall (the battle of) on page 226 is included for you!)

# ADDITIONAL THANKS TO:

Michael Miola

(For his helpful remarks on the final draft of the manuscript.)

(TYG)

# IN MEMORY OF:

MY FATHER:

FRANK FARELLO;

MY MOTHER:

ROSE FARELLO

Dad & Mom,
Love and miss you!

## *BOOKS BY FRANK S. FARELLO:*

### *NON-FICTION:*

*Changes in American Morality:*
*Of The People; By The People; For The Self*

*A Compendium of Zoom*
*(The Art Of Frank S. Farello)*

*NFT Catalog (original art by Frank Wasnt)*
*compiled by Frank S. Farello*

### *FICTION:*

*Bringing Back Balloons*

*The Rainbow Syndrome*

*A Book Of Stupid Stuff*

### *POETRY:*

*FROM FIRE AND FROST*
*(The Poetry Of Frank S. Farello)*

# INTRODUCTION

My love of writing began decades ago. My first attempts were spent writing fiction; then I added non-fiction articles to the mix. Later, once I discovered poetry, I wrote nothing else for years. I was completely fascinated by the many forms, rhythmic qualities and symbolism poetry employed to express intense feelings, ideas and the true linguistic beauty that one's prosaic use of language just cannot convey.

Poetry is timeless! Humans have written poems since the first civilizations popped up on our planet, and the emotions, thoughts and actions poetry evokes are universally understood by all.

Therefore, I offer these selections from the volumes of poems I wrote during a time of life when the cultural changes of the 60s and 70s were fading from my review mirror but, their far-reaching effects were fully felt in every aspect of daily life. For me, this was a particularly unsettling time of life as I navigated too many new realities. I found solace and direction by expressing my inner thoughts and emotions with poetry. Doing so definitely helped me better deal with many of life's uncertainties that I experienced at that time, coupled with the seeds of the global upheaval beginning to erupt everywhere; now, decades later, having grown to overshadow our entire planet as I write these words in the fall of 2023.

I have listed the poems in three sections: Altered Imagery; Hoops of Fire (a diary); Eclectic Dreams. This follows the three periods that I wrote only poetry. I stopped for a month or so after each writing period to take stock of what I had written so far and gave each section a descriptive name. Incidentally, for this book I either rewrote, updated or tweaked many of the poems to give each a contemporary tone and/or fresh perspective.

I sincerely hope you enjoy: FROM FIRE AND FROST.

Any comments or contacts you would like to make can be done through my website: WWW.FRANKWASNT.COM. Frank Wasnt is the name I specifically use for all my musical efforts and NFT art.

Lastly, any questionable spelling in the poems is intentional.


All the best,
Frank S. Farello
9/29/23

# TABLE OF CONTENTS

## *ALTERED IMAGERY:*

# HOOPS OF FIRE (a diary):

# ECLECTIC DREAMS:

# ALTERED IMAGERY

## WE ARE FOREVER!
### (To Pattie - my love, my life, my wife)

What warmth will replace

when the chill of life leaving,

leaves life without you

missing all of its meaning?

Yet, loving lets life

last beyond the last measure,

and thus through our love

we will live on forever!

# LIVING AND LEARNING

The cat jumps up,

and licks the butter

left out along

with the rest of the day,

while I kick

through the shell

of a late last night;

angle up and then out

toward the suddenly sunshine:

either living in line with my limits,

or in the cat's eclectic way.

# FOUR HAIKU FOR EARTH

Cold fingers of ice

freezing life from a sparrow -

is sorrow for all.

And the wildest weeds

are as crucial to springtime,

as every flower.

Those summer stained fields

filled with living and laughter,

still hold soldiers' graves.

And the falling leaves

complete their part of the pace -

and on, and on, and...

# GOOD GOD

Down deep in a leaf seems some silent stuff

that leaps from the lips of a smiling child,

then weaves through the breeze of a special night,

and flows from the cheeks of each trumpeteer,

to lock into life like the fingers of friends,

such substance to link every living thing's heart,

which signifies better than letters of words,

that singular flow - the good God in us all.

# TO ALL OF US, ET AL.

En masse eruptions split killing heaves, then poison mushrooms.

Item:  ice burns back the fires from freezing.

Item:  fissions of flashing breath in the end.


And when Greece and Rome, once great;

then columns of displaced marble

saved from the secretive soil; displayed

in a lesson taught yet never learned:

"Decay begins from within!"


And still of Heaven and hell we spoke

with words left crushed like soda cans,

for the past of our present future.


And again! forget the when and then;

the now:  the heaps of broken life; the global litter.

Whatever was taught was never heard,

as every day was deaf.

# TO LOSE A LOVE

Like glassine streaks of gold, light

sets sparkles in your eyes

choking twinkles from the stars.  Might

I murder me; find exile in a crack,

if cut loose from you; left hollow as a hall?


When next you chip at love, let

shards arcing down on me

quit the mutilating test.  Yet

I've questioned cars; fought smoke enough for now;

managed leaping toward the next surprising wall.


Switch starlight back to black; start

my mettle oozing rust -

could a cancer maim me more?  Part

of everything retains a part of you;

less your luster left the rest no worth at all.

# LOVE IN THE ULTIMATE END

I'm a hollow and empty space

within the world.  No longer part of

the daily continuum; like a shell

picked clean by gulls and left

to empathize with the wails of the dying.


I'm a shallow and lonely place

within the world.  Full of definite

despair; lost in the heavy haze of what's

the use, since once we were

locked in love; now never shall we meet - again.

# WHEN THE SUNSHINE WANES

Hot heat to the point wood cooks along with the waves;

slack streets ooze upward in streams of dank mirage -

then the action of the string bikinis peters out

just after the shot sand offered everything up to this Sun,

and all that was buoyant drip-dries heading home

with that tanned-out mystique puffing pride past the limits of angels,

till creamed clouds crashing in starts diehards relinquishing beach.

# ON TIME

Time ticks in a steady stream of endless seconds;

with waves detected as but brief darting moments,

each left behind in set degrees by its consent.

Neither a visitor, nor vagabond, nor friend;

mute witness to beginnings - patient till they end.

In seeking it, be aware! there is no present

                                        Time.

Who can say with certainty what Time itself intends;

what remains or wastes away, to wonder where it went?

We measure by its presence - then how it best was spent.

Most contrary condition to which all are condemned -

                                        Time.

# THE NAKED WOODS - SO SOON?

Chips spraying from the chops as cold metal meets warm wood

streak the echoes of that rhythm

with the sadness of bad memories

of children being slaughtered

for the whims of modern usage

to litter like said chips that would never turn to trees

as the increase in their number

leaves us farther from true Paradise

till someone senses rotting;

next the naked woods - so soon?

# PARALLELS

The teeming beauty of a coral reef,

links perfectly to halt the flow of ships.

A living margin reaching toward the waves;

a colony of slaves locked in death's grip.


Each generation dies, but passes on,

that oath sworn since the dawn of ocean time:

"And from these depths we'll rise and touch the Sun -

each life the base for others yet to climb!"


New strings of coral reefs still form in seas,

intent to grow and rise above the waves.

But Babel's curse extends to their domain -

they'll never rise above their liquid graves.

# CITY AT NIGHT

Exhausted and alone,

a lost lover left behind:

first accepted;

next rejected;

then goodbye -

and like a prostitute

it will give of itself

again,

then again,

yet again -

luring all into its streets;

seeking vengeance

for that

unrequited

love.

# THE MANNEQUIN

Staring into space,

glaring in the same direction;

seeming human,

never moving -

all dressed up with nowhere to go.

# ON THE OCEAN

Atop this:  all around and down below;

feeling like a young flea on its first dog,

I crave to be filled full with pure blasé -

like a Sherpa's thoughts on Everest snow.


Comparisons to astronauts afloat

upon some foreign, fluid universe,

should stifle every phobia - yet fail.

But then I think of nursing babes that swim

above those little fish kids having fun,

and realizing what a fool I am.


I've heard how coastal kingdoms come and go

(the waves just seem to scoop the land back home).

Then when it's time to live life as a snail,

at last!  I'll know what Sherpas seem to know.

# COP CARS

The sunshine starts the hum of rolling tires

lullabying me through a traveler's trance.


Then there in the distance (way back behind me);

poking at the limits of my cognizance,

an almost quiet sound gathers up tension,

then spits out a shout of loudness and light,

and pushes its madness straight into my way

in a surge of insistence bent on flooding my senses

with screaming pulsations of flashing red beeps,

till all that surrounds seems moved to confusion,

and I'm looking to zoom into some other space,

yet stretch out my patience to peak as this passes

knowing for now that the objective was elsewhere,

while bursting out swears of not one more encounter,

then STOP!

Next, settle down into the world once again,

and backtrack through patterns I've encountered before,

as the din fades away, folding into the hum.

# LIKE LIFELIKE

Every bulb burns

a hole in the night,

vying  to seem like the Sun -

but barely blocking out the Moon.


Everyone lives

a drip of their dreams,

seeking some meaning for living -

too lost in the mostly unknown.

QUIZZING BUMS

Living corners thrice removed from me:

being down, being out, being there;

so what if near the top lie past Cro-Magnons -

why the wasting rags, the worthless ways;

that fading back to dust before it's time?


Start turning 'round to see me look away,

then mutilate some other test instead.

Though abstinence from us may gain you space,

what worth is there in absolute rejection,

if living seems another form of death?

# PENSIVE TILL PRAYERFUL

Immerse me in impressions of Your fleeting glimpse,

with reflections of Your sacred image left within me;

thus that the hope of my wholly essential form

will stand poised between all the loving in my life,

and the final touch of that passing chill,

when this placard of my limitations withers,

and Your radiance resumes once we remain intimate.

# OUR SIMPLE SONG OF LOVE

To touch your heat with pure and lasting love,

then kiss, to show what now we know is real.

To see beyond the primal pleasures of,

and build upon the essence that we feel.

To think of only you throughout the day,

then pray our love is nothing less than this.

To tell each other all we want to say,

and hope to tell of things we seemed to miss.

To be two loving, caring best of friends;

to keep each other in each other's heart;

to trust, forgive, explain, enjoy, defend;

to pledge to never live our lives apart.

The only proof of everything you've heard,

is let the act speak louder than the word.

# LOOKING FOR THE LIGHT

Spaces between thoughts are still yeasting wine.

Could leafed limbs have been but roots all the time?

Is blue always said?

What use is the wish if the star is dead?

Every bird's song is just organized pops.

Turn every soapbox,

and talk of new terms for the equal sign.

Spaces between thoughts are still yeasting wine.

# BATTLE CRIES

The swollen dead sink into the earth;

for whatever it's worth - they died:

yet briefing rooms still stink with the sweat of the plan,

and killers assemble to imitate hell,

while the primary cast keeps choosing the beat;

while mothers continue their vigils for life.


Yet, suddenly someone dares offer to laugh,

and the fields swallow more of the martyred ones,

while each ancient question always remains;

while all the old baggage is properly packed.

Then though every destiny wins in the end,

it's only the dead who sigh over why.

# ONE TIME THEORY

All kinds of time exist in space,

where days occur in different ways:

a lifetime here - a second there,

and months are years, and minutes squared?

That which we really sense as time,

is relative to states of mind.

Out by the years our light has reached,

who'll understand what we call "weeks"?

Some say new life must take new forms;

what we call cold, they'll sense as warm.

Who knows, what we've passed up as rocks,

may just be men with different clocks.

# TO BE WITH YOU

Wherever you are - am I?

Wherever you choose to be - am I near?

> When the first light of dawn strikes your eyes:
>
> Am I there with you, to greet the day?
>
> Am I with you throughout the rest of the way?
>
> When those private moments relax your mind:
>
> Am I there to share that time with you?
>
> Am I part of that world you retreat to?
>
> When the day flickers out and night overtakes:
>
> Do I linger with you in between?
>
> Do I aid in your sleep, and inhabit your dreams?

Wherever you are - am I?

# WORK

Work is irredeemably dull,

        and so comparatively like nothing else,

save the proverbial old saw:  such a bore.

Still it must be done,

        and I eke it out;

                yet no more nor less than before!

# NIGHTTIME AT THE AIRPORT

A varicolored universe:

of frozen streaks of lights aligned

like soldiers left in rank and file

left guarding tracks of tar topped land

laid down for worldwide peopled birds.

Like church, the faithful flock to it

anticipating paradise

prepared for nothing more than life;

while seagulls perch above the base

to view their man-made counterparts

wondering which is their god.

# A SESTINA ON SPEECH

My mouth makes many movements,

when I stand and start to speak;

in so up-and-down an order,

lips flapping like a bed sheet

blowing in a stormy wind -

yet somehow it all makes sense.

Like a gift of seventh sense,

mouths can signal with their movements;

some have meaning, some make wind -

and what joy to hear one speak

reading from a mental sheet,

not some arbitrary order.

Mother Nature filled the order,

in an evolutive sense,

and cast aside the sheet

that prevented vocal movements.

The result:  we all can speak

of our lives, our loves, the wind.


When I listen to the wind

I feel pity, for its order

is to howl and not to speak.

If alive it would have sense

to stop and learn our movements;

taking notes down on a sheet.


Veiled in a vocal sheet,

when some talk I hear just wind,

for their mouths are making movements,

but I cannot find the order.

Since they don't make any sense,

why not simply cease to speak?


Words are treasures, so to speak,

printed on a paper sheet.

To some readers they make sense,

yet to others are just wind.

Still, whatever is your order,

just give thanks for verbal movements.


When you speak, form words not wind;

spread a sheet of oral order

making sense, not wasted movements.

# ON THE HORIZON

As often as always - there,

yet not - but seems to be;

that triple-thin seam shared by Earth and sky,

or the open wound that splits the two,

from which flows the ultra-mirage;

but above all, proof that things empyreal

will likewise lie beyond reach -

till that which will lead there is done;

till the noon of the emerald sun!

# DOUBLESPEAKING OF STANDARDS

From the ultimate confusion of everything at the end,

to the obvious implications still gathering dust,

to the perpetual attestations of that murderous maniacality

still honing that profuse guilt upon those antisemite Nazis,

to the point that the planet in stern unison swears:  "NEVER AGAIN!"


Yet, those millions - now billions of unripened fruits of the womb -

still categorized as nothing but worthless globs of true undesirables -

are wholly allied once dying from that equally homicidal treatment;

yet the questioning lingers onward and ongoing for eternities:

why the latter's demise seems never the same done by those Germans?

# SOMEONE'S MOUTHING OFF (AND ON AGAIN)

Snap it shut!

Let your lip lie so low

that the forces your seem to exert

will dissipate with the wind - never reaching the threshold of a sound;

will falter, then sink like lost fossils in the first sand;

drain away like mounds of heating snow,

to lie ignominiously like the flattened gum beneath my soles

and reveal your deepest thoughts as mere babblings -

stupid stammerings,

more useless than bird droppings in newt mud;

or more rubbish piled on rubbish;

or like putting pennies in a rich man's path,

until the very mention of your name becomes the password for asylums,

and those ideas that you've accidentally fashioned

only motivate more morons -

and your words keep meaning less - finally forgotten...forever.

# WIND SONG

If you

listen to the wind,

my love -

it speaks to you

for me;

of love

it speaks to you,

my love -

so speak of love

to me.

# MAYBE MUSIC?

Life rings with a relative resonance.

There are times I wince as it clangs,

and times I perceive it as musical.

The undulating holler of mowers -

shocking me from my Saturday sleep,

and shattering my fragile mind,

like an alarm gone out of control -

seems far from any song that's sung.

Yet, when mowers start somewhere near noon,

each effort sounds more like sad groanings,

which neither fracture or frustrate my life;

and if added to the day's symphonic melt -

I would actually consider them melodious!

## THEN COMES THE DAWN!

When the night removes its cape,

twilight signals evening's bloom.

King of Day greets Queen of Night;

day star trades with crescent Moon -

in a shadow all are draped.


Life continues without light,

where two worlds exist as one.

Most may sleep, still others rise;

then when dreams inhabit some,

kingdoms change in range of sight.


Endless time in dark disguise,

ticks on toward the daily day.

Next the night world will be gone -

to the light life it gives way,

with the shift shown in the skies.

Moving close to the morn,

slumbers slowly start to fade.

Worlds exchange as seconds pass;

lift the veil of last night's shade;

darkness dies - then comes the dawn.

Then comes the dawn!

# TO THE TIGRESS

Your feminine ferocity,

must detest the rest

through the tutelage of eons; and thus

you demand what you will of each space,

stringing victims along in a definite pace:

never least-

        never last -

                never loved.

# FEELING ORANGE

...and from that joy of the love of God,

I wear my awe like new plumage, which

ignites the varied ditches of my mind

with the flaming surge of His thrice blessed law,

turning that which within me looks toward the light

to immerse in the one, best wonder of it all;

to prepare for the flush of this new conjugation

(an illimitable found facet for what we consider as He)

while I suddenly weep out streams of true gratitude,

daring stabs at the thought: "What would Heaven be like?"

# REMINDING ME OF MY SEA

Found floating for this moment

    with lines locked to tidal space,

each boat breaks the bunching waves

    still to start its thousandth search.

Then all hands on deck unite

    like old teams of steaming bees,

wielding webs no spider spun,

    teeming toward their writhing catch.

Surely likewise through the day

    with no knowledge of the dirt,

till their move to separate

    brings them back where they belong.

Once workers line the landing,

    then the circle is confirmed:

all of life can coalesce

    since the bounty that they brought.

# AND IN THE END

Like marbles in concert

that never reach resting

your words bounce about me

to squawk of lost loving

so soon slammed to breaking

by my purely rigid

till trickling to sorry

then nail biting lonely

and mostly forever.

# PURE POETRY

words:

upon a printed page aligned,

like zigzagging strings of freight cars

full;

                filled

with someone's slanted slice of life;

switching back and forth from eye to

mind;

              touch

the idle parts of heart and soul,

with some sudden insight never

known;

            leave

behind a better, broader scope;

foster thoughts that radiate more

words.

# SOME SUDDEN SPRING FLOWERS

This day

dawned so thick with dew

that the slightest breeze,

        causes leaves

to release their liquid loads upon the land

in ten thousand sudden showers,

soaking each passerby

in a serendipitous smile

caught creasing across each face

like the spreading wake of a passing ship,

so that for now,

all else seems,

not even worth their while.

# NIGHT LUNACY

Immersed within a moonbeam's subtle stream I stand -

with thoughts in mind, and pen in hand;

in contemplation of that night light's feeble glow -

an ancient orb, yet embryo!

Most intimate companion, timeless as the tides,

and lover's crest, and mankind's guide;

a silent sentry standing on an endless post -

witness to life, yet not a host.

Then turning through the heavens for a brief repose -

another orbit to compose.

Frigid beacon - despite what you intend,

I label you a lasting friend.

## ON WITHIN FALL

Like Jack (of that beanstalk) stood poking past cloud tops,

each ashen gray skeleton sticks through this landscape -

turned bone-like by skin shed in massive, mad flakings,

till barren and stuck still mid stretching on upward,

and leaving more leaves to keep coating the dead ground,

like some soothing ointment which helps weather winter -

still proving there's beauty within every dying,

then joyous resurgence someday in the springtime.

## MERELY CHILDREN OF SOME STAR STUFF

Once, the stillness seemed almost sleepy.

Then, whatever there was:  partly this, partly that -

couldn't be kept quite together,

and the quick excitation of the atoms within

went bursting on outward, like a hot can of cola -

the spay of that ending still rains onto us all

leaving streaks of what once was within our own structure,

till the relative making of more of ourselves

incites the old ashes to rise up again,

through the foresight of Heaven's most intricate planning,

with the true missing link as the substance of space.

# FOGBOUND

So shy a rain - unsure to fall,

suspended in suspicion;

a magic veil of hazy mist,

within which all is hidden.


Ten billion pinpoint liquid drops;

a creeping wall of drizzle;

a cloud that settles on the land,

immersing all in dismal.

# SINCE THE LOVE WITHIN MY MIND

Ultimately, the mask descends,

and tributes to former days

seem culled from another psyche

while the residue of the Id drains toward its end,

and that which I never could create

seemingly leaps from me - to you,

like rays streaking to the Earth!

Then, thus being so moved,

I start the subsequence of now

initially replacing the inert,

yet so soon engaged in the best of possibilities

that I would gladly set tables for God

if the crumb being granted is to keep this exchange,

as all else is in revision, since the love within my mind.

# EPITOME

I have seen a trail of death:

twist on through the nightly news;

leaving spaces in the park;

zone out pieces of the dark;

turn the language that we use


into hushed and burning breath;

pushing everyone to fear

loving, laughing, all of life;

till the mention of a knife

causes cursing that we hear;


nearly never getting dressed,

beating every single breast.

# ANALOGOUS VOYAGERS

Then there, as chance may have it,

this intrusion (less hello/goodbye) -

from another form of midnight -

streaks like the flash of a spark's quickening wink,

to compete with this hot, heaven-lit sky;

till that instant of its subliminal passing,

when that wonder living on and within me again

switches floodings of each newfound contemplation

into references (to treasure - and forever!)

kept streaming throughout my most neural fabric's matrix

toward the one definite of every single possibility

which you yourself never seem finished searching for.

# CHANGES

Intent upon not one iota of newfangledness,

    to the point of wishing away the dawn!

Yet, even when at rest a bird could never be ignored

    by those sentenced to the dirt - for now;

but, giving in done a bit here - a bit there (wouldn't you know?)

    stalls that stagnation, for better or worse;

till circumstances trigger connections that motivate some

    to gather up wings and head for the stars.

# LOVE IN THE LAST DEGREE

Way in the back,

    in the corner,

        in the dark:

where my ears hang

like luggage;

    hands wring in despair;

lips limp

and parting,

suck in the big breeze - calling out

for you more than I would for life, and

I hope to hear,

    wait to touch,

        need to be with you -

          once more:

till this storm stumbles past, and

again I can laugh at the rain.

# THE SECRET HEART

And when one craves for lasting love -

apart from needing love,

the thought of only love,

should never crush the rest of love:

      With structures of one's own creation;

      With doors that open just for thee;

      With rooms that hold what one expects;

      With things that answer but to me -

for the finding of a lasting love,

dissolves all selfish, separate love,

and whatever was, was never love,

but the aching in one's secret heart for perfect love.

# IN A PIZZA PLACE

Swirling upward like an Olympian's discus -

and upon landing, slapping the marble slab

with much the same sound as a bolt out of the blue;

then as submissive as a martyr full of faith,

while being poked and smacked by tormentors

(worse than any pink belly ever done)

needing nothing more than might to make the change

(acting only to indulge the drooling mob).

Then smooth emergence from that fiery baptism,

with an aura that was once reserved for saints,

launching looks just like some newfound manna would

on those who chose good God's almighty will.

## OUT, MAKING OUT

Finding passion's fires burning, bursting brightly;

splitting the dark, leaving nothing left undone!

Then to lie a lot:

let the situation fade into the day;

set the recollection somewhere in a shoe;

never once to take that trip down memory lane,

only toward another place, "Some other time."

(th)ecyc  l(E)  O(f)th(e)  s(e)as  oNS

inWin  tEr'  (s)gr

ip,W  henIcesur  roun

ds,TH              efrozen  Gr  OunD

issigh  in  g.        the  ns

pr  ing(a)rrI  (v)eS;  THEtha  Wbe

gin    s,andlif(e)  A

gainis  tr(Y)            ing.insum

Mer'    sheAt, t  hebu  ds(o)b

ey;      iNf(u)l  l    dispL

aya  (r)ethr      IVing. t

hEnf  allS  et(s)in; th

ecol  (o)rschA  nGe,  b(u)

t(l)    ifere  mAi  nsbYdy  INg.

# AM I EVOLVING?

THE BEAT OF MY CONTINUOUS DREAM STATE
STILL SEEKS ITS ORIGINAL BANG!
NEXT - ALL AND IN BETWEEN, TILL
I FLOUNDERED HERE AS THIS CURRENT THING.

From singular to cellular as a sideline of Earth birth,

then a flaccid submergence in an Eden flying

through a thicker medium; and so soon a more specialized type

in random control of the niche.  Till fed up with it all,

and up,                    and out,                    and dry.

Testing each new dosage of successive surroundings with

a secretion of beginnings within range of the rest,

that just keep getting better every time...and time...and time.

Still somehow within this, my lineage is leaping!

Most finally fall silent in petals of erosion,

that hold secretly tight till the future decides.

YET, I KNOW OF MY OWN DESOLATION;
STILL GRAZE ON EACH LOZENGE OF LIFE AND,
THOUGH BEING WELL PAST AUSTRALOPITHECUS,
MY FATE AS SOME FUTURE FOSSIL
KEEPS ME BEATING MY BATTERED OLD DRUM.

# SOME SUNDAY DRIVE (THROUGH THE CITY)

In lieu of horses zip mechanicals -

sweating clean for the meantime, for the ride.


Blacktop blankets in crisscrossings like worn ribbons

shedding layers of dung, dirt, debris, dead dogs.


Mounds of remnants of once great things blister upward -

turning skylines into rows of rotten teeth.


Even wrapped within, the question overwhelms me:

"Could this really be what this was meant to be?"


Rusted tree trunks shout out placards with escape routes -

still the windows can't withhold the suffering wandering.

## OF SOMEONE IN CONSTANT NEED OF ANSWERS

My dichotomous self:

as always this or that,

then torn between the contradictions;

waits for some cleansing consciousness

to tell, with tight-lipped fervency,

whether whatever - is such,

or just hopelessly lost

in a loose knit legacy -

the value of which being moot -

and so diametrically opposed to itself.


My continuous self:

embroiled between fiction and fact,

then kept within that paradox;

left scanning for sense and reasoning

with the tenacity of steel -

though time and time again,

caught cleaving helplessly

in so precarious a position

as to render me purely useless

and continually crying out why.

# STILL JAMMED IN

Snarled in a string

of things

linked to the Fords,

within

daydreams of days

when the

roadways ran clear

in that

younger lost life,

where the

struggle was made

with much

lesser filled wheels,

which were

never replaced,

only

pushed to the point

to be

made more like life;

even

pulled into place

to show

how to live it.

# THE COLD HEAT OF MAKE-BELIEVE LOVE

With a sprawl bent more on beings than for birth,

lent like a re-offering atop an Andean altar,

for this seventh, eighth - no, ninth time today;

till your conclusion smacks of: "Someone has to do it!"

Still, the way you act (so damn convincingly):

        to feign heat, when dead cold;

        to seem loved, when near sleep,

makes one mouth out, "Why not embrace stage craft?"

which veers nearer that ultimate elation

than whatever any good (if at all) was done

lying lost in the vice that surrounds your bed.

MAN:  Having tasted this day,

and toyed with the next;

that there may well be a beyond -

I don't know!

Yet, this system retains

its primitive edge,

and my family may die out as soldiers.


WOMAN:  The feel of this pure night

spent feeling alone,

yet with your kiss upon my lips -

I now know

whatever I wasn't

never made me made.

Still, our heartbeat may stay silenced by wars.


CHILD:  What a way to play life -

running like a dog,

and everything's so full of smiles.

I still know

just why I like that game;

but then when I win,

it may never show in that other sun.

# DEEP IN THE SERIOUS DARK

Somebody's daughter died

last night.

Somebody's daughter was beat

           and stabbed

               and smashed

so bad, no one recognized her sweet face,

no more.

Somebody's child was killed

last night.

Somebody's child was butchered

           and battered;

       left broken and dead.


       But whatever is said,

would you have hung young Hitler - better yet, Napoleon?

for jonquils to be breathing better air;

for babies to be fed till full;

for reasons just to love a little more?

Then all the while stay lost like Howard Hughes,

and run on out to be a jingo each July

with pockets full or rockets

ignoring WWII, and gunging ho, and Father George:

plus apple pies, and maybe mom, and bodies in the streets!

Though this tendency seems terminal,

my penchant lies with Boston's Tea;

for pumping out prayers for better days,

and hope that for your precious kids,

that they can live a life -

again.

(special thanks to Pattie)

# UPON A PREMATURE WAKING

This crimson dawn

splits velvet skies,

soaks shutter cracks

then strikes my eyes;


rekindled life

strips me of sleep,

no chance to hide -

dawn soaks too deep;


all rest is lost -

what's done is done,

recapture dreams

when next night comes.

# SNOW FALLING

A new born storm/blizzard power blasts the settled ground for now.

Soon living is left interred and just how long will be its squeezing grip?

We've been there oh so many times before witnessing the intact impaction,

then when once done we move out on the swift attack to knock it back.


As freshly as all these flakes still seem to be, it's more the same old yarn:

we scurry 'round like panicked ants awaiting the next foot to fall fast

crushing us deeply down destroyed beneath all our glad constructions,

yet knowing full well we'll return, maybe worn but still enduring ever on.

# TURNED PRETTY PARANOIAC

Between what is and might not ever be

lie latencies that trick or tease the mind,

then turning thoughts around till things distort,

that certainly won't remain the same again.

Strange fears keep rising up within the brain

that twists the norm toward silly oddities;

raising suspicions to increasingly deep degrees

where every person, place or thing is foe.

Irrational beyond the meaning of the word;

a mental process so set against the grain,

where infinite searches never renders proof;

when every opposing thought is but a lie.

# ON AN ISLAND

This fathomless depth of this darkest deep

must yield to a peak poking through its shiny skin

which then finally first greets our mother Sun;

another lost orphan seeking its continental siblings -

those being the ancient children of the mighty mantle's force.


This most chaste bit of budding earth now born -

something like a cracker sitting still atop some soup -

dares to brave such all-encompassing loneliness

just to reclaim what we would call its God-given right:

the want to consider itself just a meager particle of land


which might soon play host to birds, bees, beasts, trees

and high hoping someday it will have a given name.

# HOOPS OF FIRE
## (a diary)

## ONLY LONELY(NESS)

Here or there,

till the meaning of myself

is the tear upon my cheek

lying lost within the rain -

then another,

      and another,

           and...

# INSPIRATIONS WHEN ON LUNCH, WHEN AGAIN EXPECTING

As our soft machines

lay loose from loving,

still basking in that basic wonder,

we reached so deep into a dream

the moment equaled mighty,

and each absolute turned vacuous -

eclipsed by this new beginning!

# TO GET BACK TO THE EGG

The action of light left too long by the brink,

set up the motion for forces divorcing

to bang out beginnings and make up this mess

(the beauty of which lies lost in the shuffle)

till doctors rev logicals back up into light;

then my matter and Venice sink into the sea,

and so on and on toward the Mighty Meld -

that one giant jumble of prodigal sons

when everyone is everything, since everything is there.

# DEEP DOWN DEEP

Having chilled (since the then

soaking ocean of losses

filled me deep, until slack, and

asleep in myself) and no sputter;

no rip-the-thought-from-my-mind syndrome;

no freaking giggle slaps me back into magical clay;

just leaving me a lump of a wasting whatever -

      sporting another burn,

      and still wanting.

# DEAR GRANDPA SEBASTIAN

When suddenly something stopped -

you left me so empty;

    so full of such loss,

    it wouldn't turn off

till I never stopped crying.


    Then things that happened since then

    fell short of sufficient,

        as life without you,

        rather than with you

somehow repressed each surprise.


        Stock shots may show what you were -

        none know the man within;

            but beyond both names,

            our minds are the same -

pure proof that you've never died!

# AFTERIMAGES

How slight the sound of your heart

once the killing glare of your only way

entered into this function!

How dead went my singular best -

to turn around like some sulking, losing thing,

then never even trying!

How fast the need for ourselves

fell away since weakened by this cut

kept between us - till always?

# ON THE FUNERAL FOR A FRIEND

Stretching the last look

till that flat snap

of the coffin

     clicking closed

amputates     your time,

          your place

          you...

then heaping my harangue

     against the wind,

since that indelible chill

sent your sentence

     to somewhere

       near starlight;

keeps freezing out my smile;

turned all things to nevermore.

# IN LOVE

Once I gave you my right sight,

you gave me your best smile;

then we lingered far longer

than each half expected,

till testing out moments

that trickled toward loving

since then - now forever,

our both being in love.

# MY CHILD

Once conceived,

you filled another place complete,

while I went on dreaming such fabulous dreams

in a glad mind mostly impatient,

yet prayerful that your being

should not lack the luster I hope

would turn back the slicker tricks

offered by those who can cloud out

the better; then burn away yearnings

by teaching you all about dreaming,

but never the road to the absolute way.

## TO ALWAYS BE

We must face each storm

with still soaking shoes

to remember the rain

and move on.

# MY DOUBLE YOLK EGG

Once my toast took chick pudding

up to my lips,

I knew that the Aztecs

killed victims in vain;

for with chicken gift giving

twice dying trying,

would anyone satisfy

gods always hungry?

# MOSTLY AT ODDS (AND ENDS)

Despite the weepy, sorry talk -

an anger stalled within your heart

that pops up pissing you off at things

I'll never seem to know or notice,

till that dirty plate turned by tantrum

to some slop spots on the wall

(when the kids would just be kids)

pushed the windows close to shattered,

like my fractured wanting/broken dreams,

left crapped out from each maximum rant.

# KEPT IN THE COLD

My own mixture cries out

as the sparks in my sound

leave leaping unnoticed

through parts of the crowd,

till scattered like fallout:

black, burnt up - then dead,

and even my motives

forgot what I've said.

# DE-HUMAN BEING

We've made pleasure our passion,

   turned tragic in love,

      till the making of more

         (like stacked books on the floor)

            tips that which we're made of,

               toward beasts flaunting all the new fashions.

# OUT OF WHACK

Just when we won,

seeming so much connected,

turning tears drained and dried

to a loving less words;

then the distance returned

till more things mattered more,

and the wanting and waiting

goes on, going nowhere.

# ON THE GROUNDS

Fields stained with stones

left standing for weeping,

each stagnant and cold,

beneath - only sleeping;

all chiseled with names

of those done with dying,

their last lonely link

with those slowly trying.

# WITHIN MY INTRICATE SLEEP

When the once rolling traffic of life left behind

swings downstream - then inward and picks out a piece

to chuck up like a clay clod reshaping at will;

plus the sand piling higher sets my mind into motion

and taps into magic made specific for night sight,

then the midsummer's tango steps into the picture,

lasting till the Sun's touch anoints the resumption

of my dying (dragging on more or less uninspired)

and/or my living returns just disguised as my dreams.

# TOO BLOCKED OUT

The arbitrary refueling of my network,

turned redundant;

offered nothing for these sheets;

left my sweat routine so ravaged,

so deep to keep me awkward -

till waiting for a hit;

and pacing;

an tearing up tools;

and starting up again - then this.

# FROM FACTORIES

A convoy of trucks' rumbles

rout out the players,

who peck at the towers

of standby replacements,

in turn filling backlogs

of long broken pieces,

half housed in old casings

that keep being pampered;

the rest making mountains

of artifacts - so soon?

# PSYCHOMOTION

Since summer lies lead-like;

and dripping down sky sap

more checks in than checks out more steam -

I'll drag me past winged things

(once fooling in puddles of sand

now switched to those drip strips)

then connect each obvious dot

to fit with my cool colored plan:

a dip in some dew till it winters!

# I'M OUT OF THE PICTURE

I've stayed too intent on my singular things:

things I do;

things I say -

all else

seems to mean zero to things beyond my Id,

while the world circles me set within certain limits;

and if pieces don't fit - then the frame is to blame,

till some caption complains of my desolate view:

so much waste;

so much want -

so underdeveloped.

# FOR ALL HEROES STILL WAITING

Since the tears;

since the fears turned to years

and the star spangled hope choked -

the matter stays stuck in the gray,

with only a Wall to remember the many,

and questions to ask for the few, who:

once weaned on the dream and the glorious cause

left marching to keep up the serious pace,

yet die every day for some discarded war;

still starve for one touch of their wonderful soil

where mothers weep vigils to kiss the man's face

of the baby who wept at the patriot's song,

and pray for some sign it will finally end:

all the years, and the fears;

all the tears.

# GEN. III. 19

Steel still peels back the long lawns

with their ripped roots reaching out

to the damned land to soothe

wounds of this latest battle lost

to that soon built thing to be standing

till some first feeble growth creeps up

winning the war man made with the Earth.

# SOMEWHAT SLIPPING AWAY

On the day I could have died:

doors that always opened wide

seemed fading into gray,

leaving locked-in all inside;

setting danger to my scenes,

with most of what I'd say

filling days too full of screams,

till decay infects my dreams.

# PASSING THROUGH PRIME

No grown gray daddy-o

still fresh from yesterday's slog

should pass the next horizon

too juiced on pseudo-youth

to writhe like a hurt worm

when everything real looping back

washes out hope of some Shangri-La;

and jamming up spaces with isolation

sours all that is left with this living.

# ALWAYS MORE YOU!

Your fluid

form still

welcomes me

                    asking

                    only to love

                    and be loved,

and making

my mind

a passionate place

                    still filling

                    with always

                    more you!

# TOO PUT OUT TO PASTURE

Living like sheep,

and that name living on

starts a silent scream-out

that there's never new motions,

till more Howdy Doody

than 4-legged fur

we keep on becoming,

to waste away birth;

too knowing next to nothing!

# HURRICANE

All polychromed light

slaved by blobs puffed to white,

lids the top of this sight

until thickened to night;

then streets cheap with room

transformed into gloom,

flush up liquefied dunes

while the wind wept monsoon;

mad torrents of rain

rush away all the maim,

then calling out names -

only silence remains

# VIVA DA VINCI

Your mind's light shines for everyone;

no point refracted through the ages.

What wealth poured onto mirrored sheets

that never doused your determined thirst!

Now the world stands still astounded:

by Sforza's horse left uncompleted;

by Lisa's styled, beguiling smile;

by parachutes before we knew;

by thoughts still stirring lettered thinking!

In spite of all we semi-seem to know,

you looked ahead and showed us where to go.

# OUT OF TOUCH

Stuck in a limbo-like temerity

left less full of here than where

once some crowded sense

meant laughing off  the cost

of this loss of mortal meaning

turned truly more naught;

 slipping from that distant now

just to want what I want!

# TOO LOSING MY LUNCH

Once wasting my mind:

this tricks up some trauma

that battles the voiding

of optimal actions,

then sports me - of sorts -

to peak more conclusive

since standardized munchings

creamed too damn disgusting,

and stretches of parkway

seem truly attractive

than iffy much longer.

## UPON A PRETTY GIRL PASSING

This pachyderm day:  draws toward

rotting out functions I've sanctioned;

kept tensions land standing

like tables and chairs at a party,

till migrating tinsel from living

when acting pure neon-like wild-eyed,

then sandwiched me zoned with such mercy,

that every said given died gladly -

killed cold by her too brilliant lips.

# BEING AT BURGER KING

Along these diurnal lines

dead faces - frozen time,

that defines the microcosm

(like approximated rhyme)

of the slack extending back

to each indecisive mind.

## ON THIS SIDE OF PARADISE

Styrofoam streams leak

along the torn land;

dead car parts still

scatter the suffering

flowers left singed by

the wind from the choked

bloated river too lost

under clumps of sheaf

treated trees still

screaming once headlines

like someone should care;

while my mind begs the sky

till my eyes stain the dirt,

as I've never felt so less

angelic.

## WITH YOU ANEW

Near my mind once my head screwed straight

lands your excellence sparkling up spaces

with an instantly delightful luxury

leaving lengths of your smile within everywhere,

and the brightening light streaking your eyes

whips up new patterns of exalted withdrawals

till I'm racing through pages for shouting expressions -

then the known:  TO BE ONLY WITH YOU!

# IF NOT VIRGO

To those tweezing out perfection

from the hostile swamp surrounding -

though your virtues seem inspired

all the others must see vices,

for the slack of piss poor reasoning

can't dare fill scattered spaces,

nor initiate one angstrom

on toward action less the babble,

and more mass procrastinations

just contribute to the wasting,

until the circle that's invented

spins on round and round in place.

Best attempt some sense of order

than such absolute stagnation.

# AT THE ASYLUM

I streamed past tiers for demented sons;

for mad, crawling daughters of anyone,

left lost in the nights of their separate days,

till the shells of themselves leave all that remains

to dangle in limbo like walking on thin ice:

most waiting to tumble back into the earth;

some standing from not having given up hope.

# STILL HOLDING ON

Till you

take my hand,

to touch

seems more

some insufficient

tactile chore.

Yet, if

you would live

in love

with me,

each touch approaches

destiny.

# ONE SUDDEN WAY

...and the surging burst of each mountain slipping;

         more backyards churning,

wiped away fashions till paisleys turned precious.

Then blood stains on wreckage matching cheap chocolates

made thoughts of long Liebfraumilch weep tears from my eyes

when old wizened wheat things seemed tragically scrumptious.

Those warping fence remnants could serve as a table!

Has anyone offered to smile over lunch?

Please show me a fork,

and a plastic St. Francis to lean my mind on.

Now the mortgage will never be due,

yet I'll dream of ten paths of gardenias,

and my gray, lightweight, summer tuxedo.

Oh, would brown mustard go with those wheat things?

Here, have my last hotdog for one taste of your toothpaste -

take any seat for the joys of last Christmas!

# RAIN REIGN

New orphaned sky

pieces particlized down,

in death defying diving

splattering the split spaces,

objectively drowning out

the day's dreaming, again -

more sovereign than Royals

as everyone gets wet!

# ALL OF YOU (ME)

We caress to kiss,

till each the other

is only this;

then all of you

is all of me;

alone - unknown,

together - to be.

# HYMN FOR HER

In your infinite light

(more than pretty is pretty)

thus drinking the darkening

most of my make-up,

till absolute magic

is every tomorrow,

turned dreamlined living

meant only for you.

# IMPASSIVE

Once we rival:

she kills me so soundly

my affinity flows more like ink-puking squids

        than thundercaps clapping,

and each dawned night thereafter

        keeps cheapening our needing;

fully forcing our actions,

        till with no one too happy -

she should catch her particular breath

        while I could turn out truly pedestrian.

# DISTORTIONS

Once simply wood

      bent on staying the same,

then extending from someone

          to execute slaughter,

then tricking the trees

        to feel truly guilty,

and all of our unborn

        to carry the blame;

like the whack of the whip

         must always be faulted,

for maintaining the suffering

          life of a slave.

# ONWARD TOWARD INWARD

My chips lie low,

blaming:  fire for frost;

      winning once losing;

or infinite pages of probables -

and as always my ambiguous smile,

but never my own contrition!

# EVIDENCE OF AFTERMATH

Some solidifying sky strike,

storms more toward lead-like

unzipping a swarm of undisciplined stingers

to stab the insouciant and effortless Earth

with a tentative attack of unlimited light,

till the tension expended snaps back into nesting,

while the land bleeds the stains of such ultimate rain.

## APPLES AND ORANGES

You're a better person than I deserve.

Then we he said/she said all day;

play our harps just to make more noise;

slam some draws just to weaponize sound;

watch dumb shows just to seem less desolate;

spout out steam till our clocks tick down -

then switches flip, and we compress:

better braced for the next sign of frost.

# FEELING DOWN

As I am always to be here,

yet now more set within this glum

than the suddenly dead still grieving

over all their memories too lost

to only the living left sad

and forever surrounded by rain.

# WE'RE HITTING THE SKIDS

One too

      many times we've

fractured apart, to

          botch up

               the action of

our ultimate loving, till

             washing away

all best we could do

           with nothing

but footsteps

      to live past

the snow.

# STILL MIXING ME UP

With my living came thinking

with more spouts too chaotic

till so close to conclusions

that so seemed like great endings

each piece of my reasons

left answers so mangled

that no explanation

calmed my curious soul.

# ON EVIL'S EMPTY PROMISES

While you're screwing your wishes in place

there sounded out promises (all hope coated nothings)

each choking each lesson with saccharine dreaming,

so blinding the sight that we still barely see -

save the tears dripping down, so daily down -

proving wretches fare better less turning your way,

and the depths of vile living seems wasting the space,

and your touting your domain leaves everyone sinners.

# ONCE WE TOUCHED

It's this instance of our vital space,

    that moves us like two skipping stones,

        to reach beyond as each exists,

            so fervently for the deepest in us

                to secure the eternity of time -

                    to be together forevermore.

# EACH AN EMPTINESS

This graying day

turned the slate toned sky

to a roaming storm

looking for a place to cry.


While every flash

of that intricate force

soon brings puddles of pieces

for all that was lost.

# LIVING LIKE ONION-LIKE

Each peeling away

    of a leaf

        of a lily;

reveals the decay

    of the grief

        of that killing.

# LOST WITHIN A LOOP

Sent sandwiched

between the supportive buoys of this day

together with the vacillating renditions

that underline

the evident obligation

that now circles about

like any turnstile lumbering beneath the City's streets -

this dichotomy seems

most appropriately baffling

as I've done this repeatedly

for what dreams like eternities:

continually caught within the revolutions

that so often contain,

but could never define any direction taken,

less the said mechanism

calling out an absolute ending of this stall.

# IN SEARCH OF STARS
## (a double sestina)

<u>An introduction:</u>

And God created Heaven and the Earth;

then He lit the fires of the human mind.

Our ancient ancestors were first to know,

the heavens were alive with points of light.

They stood and stared with wonder in their eyes,

that gift of intellect the driving force,

and with critical thinking dared ask why.

This is the legacy of modern man,

from stone age artists painting shooting stars,

to what we know today of outer space.

That drive was always in us from the start;

the hungry mind of man will always think.

<u>The age of the unknown:  Prehistoric Man</u>

The caveman's basic logic made him think

strange beings seemed to dwell above the Earth,

or spirits freely floated 'round the stars.

To solve this matter, where would he then start?

He knew the day depended on the light,

but could never understand how or why;

the reasons were beyond his tribal mind.

This so perplexed and puzzled ancient man -

so frustrating to see and want to know -

yet, answers remained lost in outer space.

The caveman's rationale of cosmic force:

all things were types of gods before his eyes.


The age of speculation:  The Egyptians

From rafts upon the Nile man turned his eyes,

to stare at desert nights and often think:

"Somewhere out there is some almighty force

that set the time when every star should light."

This thought alone drove men to question why,

and how this had impacted life on Earth?

If gods were out there then they would not mind

if somehow all the rest of us would know,

what was that force; what is the use of space?

The answers lay somewhere among the stars.

Their thoughts were only but a simple start.

That force controlled the destiny of man!

The age of investigation:  Ancient Greece

On entering the golden age of man,

we see the stars through ancient Grecian eyes.

Again, the hope is just to answer why,

and understand that universal force.

Greeks felt the Earth was central to all light.

This geocentric theory, they did think,

explained the movement of each orb in space.

Despite advancements of the human mind,

there was much more that we wanted to know.

One thing the Greeks had proven from the start:

The more we learned of space could aid the Earth,

and someday we might fly among the stars.

## The age of theology:  Christianity

And now the Christ descended from the stars

to spread the words of God to every man.

He spoke of one eternal sacred force,

which flows through Heaven, Earth and all of space.

He taught that God created man and Earth,

and of the powers of the human mind -

but not to dwell on petty reasons why

the planets spin, or how suns shine their light.

He knew we had a ceaseless need to know;

would always use our intellect to think;

would always search the heavens with our eyes -

but warned, never forget God was the start.

## The age of superstition:  Medieval Man

Down deep in castle keeps did research start,

143

born from the myths surrounding all the stars?

While most still ruled their lives by cosmic force,

others preferred to know and study space.

New science sought out origins of light;

astrologers said stars affect the mind -

so here we have new thinking asking why.

This revolutionized thought on the Earth.

Religion prescribed what each soul should think,

since what pleased God was partly known to man.

As questions surfaced, some shifted their eyes,

craving answers to what they did not know.


The age of intellect:  The Renaissance

Beliefs would change as men sought more to know

of laws existing always from the start.

The universe was there, but when and why?

What use was life, and what of mortal man?

Renaissance people trained themselves to think,

of nature's laws in and around the Earth.

No question was too sacred for one's mind.

What answer could explain the realm of space?

DaVinci's mind and Galileo's eyes

probed deeper into nature's cosmic force.

As Tycho, Kepler cataloged the stars,

still others tried to set the speed of light.


The age of understanding:  1650 to 1750

With intellect the guide, next came the light!

Now everyone alive wanted to know

'bout planets, comets, moons and distant stars.

First, Newton wrote of gravitation's force;

then Martian features dazzled people's eyes.

Soon moons were found around ringed Saturn's space.

 Next, fiction space tales spread across the Earth.

This wondrous age feared not to question why.

It fostered and persuaded all to think.

Past generations could but only start;

here we see the rise of reasoning man

affirming all vocations of the mind.


The age of discovery:  1750 to 1850

Each new announcement boggled every mind!

When Herschel confirmed dawns of double light,

existing past the range of human eyes,

his finding flashed across the awestruck Earth.

Telescopes trained up in our drive to know.

Once comets revealed their secrets to man,

instantly arose countless questions why.

When asteroids zoomed into local space;

and sunspots seemed to swim across the stars;

and math was deemed the law right from the start;

and Verne, with pen in hand, forced us to think -

before men flew, Earth had its first Space Force.

The age of progress:  1850 to 1950

At Kitty Hawk the effort went full force -

now nothing was beyond the human mind.

Next, rockets would attempt to reach the stars,

and answer everything we yearned to know.

No longer would this planet confine man;

soon we would break our bond to Mother Earth -

our efforts were more how instead of why.

First photos of the Moon found eager eyes,

and lured us even deeper into space.

Vast distances were set in terms of light,

then Einstein spoke and showed us where to start -

his space/time theory changed the way we think.

The age of adventure:  The Modern Era (1950 to the present)

With Sputnik's launch the world began to think

that space was more than just some unknown force.

It seemed to be a future home for man,

whose rockets pierced the early morning light.

The more we learned, the more we hoped to know.

Soon men beheld the Moon with their own eyes.

This huge step of our journey to the stars

filled humans with a drive to conquer space.

What followed would amaze the ancient mind,

as Mars and Venus next played host to Earth.

These modern triumphs only were the start,

to answer our most ancient question: "WHY?".

The age of analysis: The Future

We search for alien life - if none, why?

Surely we're not alone, we choose to think.

The space age struck with such a potent force -

still, more answers remain for us to know.

The future of our race lies with the stars.

Though we've already made a noble start,

massive efforts still lie before our eyes:

erect a Mars base to colonize man;

 build way stations that rise by lunar light.

These tasks will further tax the human mind.

What point in time moved man to survey space?

 When God created Heaven and the Earth.


Conclusion:

As long as we still think of life in space,

the destiny of man is in the stars.

As long as we ask why suns shine with light,

we'll always need to know if God's the force.

As long as man and mind exist on Earth,

whatever quest we start opens our eyes!

# UNDER YOUR OVERWHELMING ME

The quicksand

    cliffs of your

        ebony eyes,

sink me

    too deep

        in the rest of

            your mystery,

to pull me

    toward needing

        not much

            of myself;

toward being

    devoutly

        devoted

            to you.

# ASKING SOME QUESTIONS

Should we love

such that we rust the other

worn away -

too doomed to loathing life

to see a silly cloud,

till no memories flow,

no season stands apart

with melodies of loving aloud,

till the sight of the other's smile

glows like an ugly spark,

lighting the depths of the way

toward nothing?

# A PRAYER OF PROTEST
## (to all the Boomers)

Once we filled up this space

and weathered our changes

we set out en masse

to fix up the future.

Now, we live in complacency

with our focus diverted

till the parts left within us

did naught for our children,

and the darkness returning

just boosted confusion;

and we're groping at random

for just one of those whispers,

as everything slopes back

well into the mainstream;

and more true tribulations

leaves all losing salvation,

as our daily contentment

of our suburban commitments,

leaves prayers falling exhausted

with a bitter taste lingering,

and not one explanation

for our dropping the ball.

# TO ONE POOR BABY DOLL TRAPPED

The opposite prink of your devastating skin,

spared my glad fancy to deduce the design,

till I climbed up to quench on your super-sheer smiling;

then velveteen eyes steaming subtle contempt,

clicked off my ogle that favors your angle

half borne by the rut of homogenized men,

yet fueled as you trade off those ultimate charms

still seemingly leaving you cold, empty arms.

# YOUR YOU
## (if she would write)

Your you would never make me,

but open up and break me;

take away much more of me

than I could ever stand -

please keep your potent promises,

then leave my love alone;

your you remains more everything

I'll never need to know.

# UNDERWHELMED

I'm evading the places of old mausoleums;

their quick sapping wasting

meant for dumbing us down.

With their myopic walls - all intrusion proof structures

of shortsighted contentions

still left covered in drool.

Their calamities scatter like the cold flight of dead leaves

while their halfhearted sentences

contain no further use.

Then, many spent splattering their cacophony of excess;

now, silent and rattled

by the coming new Moon.

# ECLECTIC DREAMS

# TILL SINKING IN

Life is like sand -

and my days grew too liquid;

then the penance of being

dreamt dead expectations;

and each day I'm absorbed

in more signs of disruption.

# TOO PIECES OF PIECES

Trash the battered, strained equations;

chuck the miles of moldy mumbling,

till the truth embracing all

lets the dead retreat from breathing

like the living streak about

toward immaculate vacations,

and this line-up for eternity

scraps the weight of past assumptions

for that final restoration with the angels!

# FRESH HELL

Just to jar myself

    left lost upon a shelf,

        till the label lifts

            falling flat onto the floor -

along with my intentions

    that fade so far away,

        like the wasted days

            of my newly closed doors.

# FRANKLY SPEAKING

When given a given,

        some insatiable spot

in my too being human

        must slop up that gospel

till I'm full of the facts

        and left leaking all fiction -

then the testing resumes

        at that definite pace,

or sinks back with boulders

        while I'm laughing and lost in a theory.

# FROM VACANT ROOMS

Even after

the looking light swings

ringfuls 'round parts

of the darkness,

and this new, brilliant view

left blanded

by blue loops of

a more keenest truth

slipping me jinxed news

of long wonderful whens -

then this sudden, tough

tearing down thing wears away

links with a song, and

some used news even opens

these doors a full bit,

leaving the likeness more luminous,

yet left tipping on toes

till the full fires return -

for another go at the effort.

# GONE FROM THE GARDEN

My steely smile loped toward losing pure cheer,

once born bound by the most down

of these things the mind might find,

till the trickling slices of clipped laughing

stand for a life more like fondling a flame

once the floating smoke

chokes each iota of time

and there won't be much dancing anymore - till eternity?

# A WORLD WITHIN

Being poor in the park sets

the latitude on aching, and

the symmetry of dawn more

a treacherous engine that

groans as it swells at

snapping out living, then

thundering away to

talk about dying.

# TO THE NEXT NOAH
## (upon hearing of floods)

With the wet sand

    comes the dead life -

those lost to more suffering:

    who'll molt their last union

with groups left migrating;

    whose muted insistence

screams out, "Angels forgot us!";

    who turned newly distant

feeding fits of the landscape.

# PENCHANT TO HOWL

The obligatory                     blaring                     beat...

of the curt cruisers in heat

inflames the drained streets

with the dogmatic wail of hard rubber,

till the tracks of their standardized zigzags

trips the trigger of one amplified opposite

toward the intersection of now and infinity,

then the night shrieks out synchronous sirens.

# AT THE PARK

What a breeze

that drags the ridded beer cans

growling grievously

over such a sudden descent into uselessness,

then their bunching back and forth

like panic-stricken survivors

too losing points to this cataclysmic action;

then so soon snatched by factions

utterly tuned in to this adversity

that they barter on for hours

and pray for a continuous breeze.

# NEW TOTEMS

Poles line the sad scene

long linked through a listing

of more probable forces

than ever were stacked

on those Indian sticks;

still the action remains

in complete continuity

though all the gods' voices

strayed too far from the phones.

# BACK AT THE PARK

The last long steps

lean toward

the trim trees

then back to the wrong world,

while the essence of the Earth

that I so wish to retain

is in all

that surrounds me.

# DEAR DARLING
## (to Pattie)

My love,

You leave me more molten

than wild undulant flowers

scream-teased by heat's fabric

from some passionate wind,

till the true sparkling touch

of your infinite heart

ignites me long electric

and burning with being.

                    Your love.

# MAKING MINE MONOCHROME

My very verve rings eclectic!

Yet, new unknown nouns fling impingements about

like some pitching machine in a panic

wound to trouncing my optimum bliss,

till vague gray days creep in too deeply,

and my housing becomes mostly their home.

# IN MID-SEPTEMBER

I will always know

that the Sun's light easing me on,

at this moment on my face

by the shoreline where I stand,

dissolves away the fleeting real -

till the more I'll think of you

locks the links within our hearts

like new water birds flying together...forever.

# ALMOST ALWAYS

As steep

  as the wild waves

       seem swelling

      like young hills, till

     made melting

back beneath,

  and too soon losing

  touch with some

        penultimate sky

  in favor of the deep - my

desiderate  dreams

     seem less

everlasting than

   the need to

  dissolve away

into sleep.

# RIPPLES

Each toss of a stone

        sent toward the unknown

extends the effect

        of the waves we reflect

till the action of time

        erases the lines

and whatever was found

        sinks silently down.

# BIG CITY DYING

Well worn,

yet long belonging -

these suffocated streets

still dip with the steely weight

of every damned dawn,

once the reams of steep living

land crammed by the brutal fate

of every extreme effort

having been so saturated

by such appalling degrees

of excessive wane.

# TOWARD TWILIGHT

This stiffening Sun

still licks at my motions

till the soon sleeping beating -

like a contrary fire -

seems freezing

my mind up

this time.

# DOWN DROWNING AGAIN

My thickening laughing

        caught me most cold -

then one wallowing surfaced

        to parch up more memories,

and some signal went blinking

        to blank out the questions,

and my final intention

        turned to liquefied doctoring,

till all this day's damned renewed cruelties

seemed so soothed - if just until tomorrow.

# CAPTURED IN COPIAGUE

One rough red storm of stop lights

sliced this day too deep into myself;

wilted away the residue of some best dreaming,

that that glimpse of the torn, still sadness

so stained my way; so set me lost within each why,

that for the sure safekeeping of my cherished self,

my quickening departing pointed me well into tomorrow.

# RESOLUTION ON EVOLUTION

So long so caught and contained

      within rude hunks of wasted space, once

      the slack sacked the truth, and

      new roots seemed left littered

      in some oozing life;


too long too used to the teased needs

      then never somewhat knowing, as

      the pace dripped on demanding, and

      each sound sold hollow outtakes

      still missing the mark;


how long how much more those stages

      dreamt their delusions about us, then

      suddenly spouted no meaning, and

      then the only way needed

      was there all along.

# PROTRACTED ANONYMITY

There,

where the dark

accumulates most;

where the deepest frost

so brittles

the lessening light

that stars' twinkling

is nevermore.

Thus,

will all things

shatter away

once being left

lost within

the ubiquitous

unknown

of transience.

# VENGEANCE

The             watchful waves

keep         extending their reach;

their     vigilance behaves

like       the patience of sleep,

and when all wears away

then their plan is complete.

# MORE WARRING US AWAY

Still, helicopters stand

        landing

then split their big bodies to

spill out more of the green ones, who

plant,        then slant away

dancing amid discharge

that maims and drains away

futures of possible genius modes,

and/or simple times among picnics

flowering on the sidelines of the world;

now replaced with the screaming of some

saving their being; some falling upward toward

the heavenly slopes; some dazed and torn and broken,

as others enter to gather the remnants, and replenish the field

for the reaper always found riding about.

# FRAGMENTATION

While dying - I'll supper,

and pick at the pieces of

some broken sad furrows

etched deeply within the layers

of thick residual thinking

that seemingly lingers untoward

for the duration of this timeframe;

then an incompleted moon

leaves all this lost in my pockets

till the next fragile daytime

shatters right into place.

# GREETING CARDS

And again, this thing seems such a chore

as some splendid pages lost their joying.


Last Christmas every line seemed stained

with echoes of our heated words;

next, birthday ways of wishing you

leaned more involved in what we are.


Still, I teeter between the should or shouldn't

asking, "Do those authors in their ideal places

expect pure clients for their treasured efforts?"

Rather, somehow each has surely known

the lengths and depths of our giving, and

just how much I'll always love you.

# ONE SUCH PLACE?

Friend,

    is there

        one such place

where the vapors of the past

leave no trace -

        no taste,

won't stretch out

choking  time with a full fretfulness

           that lingers

in corners

clogging the freshness of air

with the fumes of atrophy?

    Is there

        one such place

where the purity of the heart

will project out an

excited now

living less the yoke

of long reminders and the infinite rehashing

of whatever was?

Friend,

is there

one such place?

# UNTITLED (A)

At the downward dip

    of the evening warmth

when my mind selects no boundaries,

my face forms reflections

        in the deepening sky

till I stand so far away from my shadow

        that my lifetime

leans forewarned.

# OPTIMAL DREAMING

At the opening of this wide night,

I soon stashed my most accurate trapeze,

and left without a cup of tomorrow

toward such chemical downstairs things.

First, the feelings were somewhat more floral,

then I settled upon milking creation

as the white wind kept on partially talking,

and half of my laughing leaned crimson

once my patience stayed steeped in an autumn.

I found formed ultimate oceans of gladness

which swelled as the august land shrank,

yet the small slenderest mention of anything

boiled me back for my absolute freezing,

though increasing my fine tuning my incidence

left me wrestling with questions of wandering

as these things that kept blistering sleep

forced me flouncing for another condition

that would render me turning more nuanced.

Dragonfly,

      dragonfly,

shut down

      your wicked

            wings,

and remain among

            those planted things

to let

      your day

            flow by;

don't bother

      with more

            notions

of to buzz about my space,

lest my pace

      turns toward

                    annoyance,

    then

        I land

            you

                crashing

                    down.

# THE UNDERTOW
## (to our unborn Bridget Rose)

Some still too deep grip of damned death

last reached for these multiple shores

and flushed our new budding new garden

just to wash away someone we loved.


Still, the cold dips clean down to the marrow

when so thinking of things left undone,

and how lost from our arms and forever

once your true birth was something eternal.

## A TRIP TO ANTIQUE TIMES

All the magic mirrors have been spent,

trying to appease the need for a resumption,

yet each long-lasting day means additional same

from that stack grown increasingly dear,

but the aimlessness of the withering

stands most like long racks of worn meat

left out drying in the sun for the flies!

# ALWAYS SOMETHING TO DO

My moves reek of infinite finishes.

Still, the details lean never saturated,

and most latches seem keep popping open,

till my engines scream running around

more establishing lists after lists,

like I'm spooning raindrops from the sea!

# COLD DAYS FORMING

The dead have wed,

and the trees strip down in celebration,

then that freezing grinds onward;

creaking like a long rolling behemoth,

choking out beauty beneath its traction

so that all we can do is listen

for the all clear bells dawning

severing us from inside this aching atmosphere.

# FUNERAL PROCESSION

Long locked in mourning

on some worn out fashioned trail

aimed at someone's architect's

finely tuned stack of stones

where every passing sad ego

does land itself eventually

within that week's rainbow's dead end,

while we still think back and forth,

staying so strung out on the same,

born from all the freshness of that green grave.

# BENEATH THE BLUE SUBURBAN SKIES

From some last, long utopia

streams the first saddened penitents

cast out from some former Main Street

through all the faults of their own,

and their dead, plastic duck-like things

will forever litter all the trim lawns

while that wasting of this place

bogs down all those hypocritical lives.

## LEFT SPEECHLESS
### (a long lesson learned)

Within an all too true landing zone

less one more serious saved space

seemingly torn from some deepest infinity;

would that this too lean bounty would talk,

then my new chosen long link in the chain

would involve the spirit of everything,

and my always in need of reminders

would be framed and then nailed to a wall,

left reverently touted as some excellence -

yet, never fully functioning as such

till there shows really nothing was there

save some picture of a place with no name.

# ONCE THE FIRST TEN THOUSAND THINGS DONE

In a place such as this

(once some seasoned living)

every mention was made,

and the answer is giving;

now the balance begins

(with whatever was said)

and those absolute answers

must sustain me till dead.

# BROKEN DOWNTOWN

Sad,

stained,

black stacked

extended things

sent to plot the deeper spots

of torn cumulative time;

our emaciated prime;

left to join the long lessons

of our wanton persistence.

# LEFT KEPT IN A RED WINTER
## (11/22/63 - 11/22/23)

The exit wounds still stink

as our longest loss - so far,

jams my bowl of Trix - back then

with the eggs and toast - right now;

and those every fuzzy pictures,

and more horrid film of films

of that very scuzzy story,

turns each sterile load of questions -

still re-fathomed since pre-Beatles -

toward more tears expecting answers,

yet things still dragging on and on

seems to have been the plan anyhow.

# FROM A PICTURE

So screwed into this chair

while gnawing at an apple

caught by a view of yore

to the hoot of my year ten,

and my laughing links me back

as I'm still standing by the shore

somewhat sensing the unknown

within the measure of my mind,

then I'm back among the now

when some thousand words describe

what I think things should have been.

# DURING A DRY SPELL

When settling down to contemplate,

something chucked the penned poetics

laying waste to more new rhyming;

plus the said is already at rest,

and the coffee stained dead stock

seems repentant in their racks.


The next steps contain the future,

and just how many more I'll manage

giving life to in the new plethora,

and while some absorb old piffle

dreamt to signify new passion

I'm melting into regurgitated words.

## OF YOU AND I TRYING

With each dream left unlatched;

left too loosely fulfilled,

we would empty our eyes

and shout out for more rain,

then smear every memory,

till it's yesterday once more!

# STILL TRYING

The same sound

of our wounded hearts

still mending,

flows translucent

through those shadows

meant to always be

left behind us

and forever.

This tendency

so infinity alone

sustaining us

will continue on

within our dreaming together,

always and as long as

we're steadfastly there

still trying.

# SUCH A SAD SYSTEM

This infinite beating of brains

of the worldwide formal nouns

barking daily mumbo jumbo

lest more mushrooms pound the ground,

smacks of silly lists of smearing

driving the running of these things

since we've abandoned all the trees

and until we pulverize this place,

then this primitive space we've made

will dissolve and drain away

and the supremacy of ourselves

becomes the basis for more dust.

Almost always

        when something leaves me

        there is nothing

to expect from me

        that would contain the same,

        or cause me to even show;

then when some dreaming

        explains the difference

        then the "almost"

turns to fleeting

        and the "always"

        I just hope to never know.

# DEEP NEEDING YOU

You've soaked me more immersed

in what expectations follow

once the glistening of things

dancing dazzled with your wonder

turns toward scattering the bunches

of my stunted cold conclusions

then the dream of living loving you

puts me part of us forever.

# STILL SKIMMING THE SURFACE

Each widening trail

        of life's new laughing tears

seems the smiles meant for that

        fronts another contention

when the source of the joyful

        bends things further away.

Then the mention of such

        turns the tension to sighing

once whatever is found

        leaves some questioning linger,

or new thinking contains

        more confusion for both?

# TREATING IT TENDERLY

We speak so much of being in love,

yet know so little of the depths of attention,

or the specialized nature of commitments to one.

Yes, the smiles in the sunshine after a passionate kiss

is a living dream; a rapturous experience,

still we often proceed to the next event

without understanding how extraordinary that was,


nor the flow of creation set within each heart,

nor the lengths of tenderness that pour through the soul,

sustaining our existence well into eternity.

The treatment we craft for the other we love

expands from the innermost parts of the heart,

from attention paid to every aspect of that love

making each life experience so suddenly authentic,

and the pace of reality worth more than the now

as we focus our heart on how better to love.

# FROZEN GHOSTS

The so many warriors spent on pushing agendas

would have better been left  just plowing their fields;

could have better been taught to curing all cancers.

But the powers that be thought nothing of that

when they forced all that life to form hills of such death,

sheer fodder and fuel for their goals then and forever

an unending machine of dying, death, destruction

still littering the pages of our historic journals

a dark stain of our nature that craves to conquer

no matter the sadness, suffering - such sorrow,

and the hands left lifeless and sinking into the soil,

and all the lost seasons spent less all the laughter,

and the lives left uprooted to never recover,

and the places of memory where they only remain,

and the flashes of living set frozen in time...forever.

# POST TRIALS AND TRIBULATIONS

...am almost home now -

and in a way so wonderful

that my anticipation turns this way

being only back into your arms

the continual cause for more of that

after day after day after day

knowing all the lonesome while

we want what is forever ourselves.

# LOST THOUGHTS

These thoughts that hang on losing life

stem from the gripe of a cryptic piece

that ebbed and flowed through my innermost

to trick this drain on my every part

away from that which I think of myself

till I'm set to forget any most of me

for just a morsel of how much time is left.

## ALWAYS A CHOICE

Why do we forever so soon abandon

things all away; then quick

move on toward an empty-

ness; and stay lying back

denying every single best; too

lost and too alone within the dark to feel;

        deny the need for tenderness and touch-

           ing; no uplifting, only longing

             kept treasured and dear and

              deeply set; to express less

              measures of our emotions;

            ignoring the need for more affection?

# HOW OFTEN DOES IT SEEM THE HONEYMOON WANED?

The bed stayed unzipped

when the scars left upon it

meant even needing some sleeping

was some venture beyond it.

# UPON REACHING THE BEACH

Such tall sparkling eyes

shining brighter than the Sun

with you still looking so good

dazzled me long, at long last,

that the thought of the rest

streaming both in and around

left their flashing disjointed,

and their hollow games empty

staying so wrong for so long

makes your increasing gladness

just all that must matter - to me.

# NOT BURNING DOWN THE HOUSE

With the mean

fading fast

then both you and/or I

seem still squeezing out tears

of continuous atonement,


then the last great unmentionable

sets up to shatter this place,


yet our gathering fires

smolder down into smoke

flying so far away

toward the Moon.

# TO MY FIRSTBORN SON FRANK
## (love you)

Frankie's in!

And that sweet, gleaming face

sent more daylight in motion

once ten tunes of each happening

fills all corners of silence.

Then his happiest strong songs

switched the moment to magic

when some fun fueled dimensions

teamed to gather up living.

I would wait in amazement

for his next glad appearance

when he taught me more lessons

that I thought I had known.

Now I look at the passing

of so many new journeys;

I've learned more from you

more than anyone I know.

To the man there before me

with that sweet, gleaming face:

there's such comfort in knowing

that you've always been here.

# TO MY DEAR DAUGHTER EVAMARIE
## (love you)

With your gifts always giving

in the trust of your hugging,

and your laughter in living

every ounce of the time;

then the streams of your dreaming

lifted my flat occupations

with a magic that made

your next smile feel like mine.

Within you always showed

the special in everything

that all others seem missing

or were left never to know.

It was always in the daily

when watching you growing

on toward all that you were

so fruitfully meant to be.

The ebb and flow of life

brings the tides and the times,

and there are chapters of your living

I know are still yet to flow.

# TO MY SECOND SON SEAN
## (love you)

Just when time seemed to stop,

and the world seemed so empty -

on the day of my beginning

you entered this place.


While I think of your daring,

and adventures on the fringes,

I could never have known

which way things would have gone.


I know I said this way,

but you moved more toward that way!

I'm sure that's the way

it was just meant to be.


So, here we are now

both well past those episodes,

and I'm just so thankfully glad

for the way you have grown.

So the cycle of living

turned round one more circle,

and here you are as I was

thinking of the best that will be!

## LOVE POEM TO MY ANGEL, MY WIFE PATTIE
### (I deeply love you and am always yours)

Your long standing laughter

went waking my deep sleeping,

so electric and uplifting

to my terrible blasé;


then the shining, the sparkling

from such eye-filling gulps -

my connection went critical

needing touching more tenderness;


but if gone from your company

and the singing and joyful

life would drain from my dreaming,

and what else would I do?

# QUADRINALL
## (the battle of)

(I)

Echoes of distant fanfare and rumbles -

a dog lifts its head and angrily grumbles.

The peace of the forest will be troubled today,

for men will do battle in a bloody display.


Shielding its face from this vile demonstration,

the Sun casts dark shadows in retaliation.

The foxes and rabbits cringe together in fear,

for the air smells of death as the battle draws near.


Far to north a Red army approaches,

while south of their course a Black force encroaches.

Both aim to settle their questionable brawl

on the green hilltop all call Quadrinall.


King Allerdale leads the well trained Red forces,

behind him his choice knights ride high on their horses.

Each soldier is silent as he ponders his fate -

to die or survive no one can stipulate.

The Black troops are headed by Hegemont the Cruel

whose credentials include a tyrannical rule.

Though loyal his troops may be to his reign,

each enters the battle for personal gain.

Bearing maces and swords and other grim weapons,

each army feels confident they'll teach the lesson.

Every soldier has mastered some sort of skill -

on horse or on foot they are trained in swift kill.

The future of freedom will be decided today,

for under Black rule no one has their fair say.

King Allerdale knew this was the only recourse,

since for years the Black foe tried to conquer by force.

Oh, Quadrinall with trees so tall,

so undisturbed from spring to fall.

When morning comes and dawn's light buds,

　　　　　your fertile soil will be soaked with blood.

(II)
The pace of the marchers beats like a drum;

the ground vibrates rhythmically with a deepening hum.

Every man in the ranks seeks a swift victory,

and return home a hero to his friends and family.


Through the thickening brush each army must trudge,

chopping down all that won't give way or budge.

By midday the armies reach the foot of the hill,

then initiate plans for an effective kill.


King Allerdale signals for his archers to start,

with a salute they draw arrows and then depart.

Next, he commands his brave knights to begin,

and behind these forces the foot soldiers join in.


As Allerdale watches, his brave army moves out.

"Godspeed!" he whispers then ponders his doubts.

So many good men he must send to their doom,

but the fate of their homeland dispels all his gloom.

Now Hegemont has also prepared all his men,

and in similar fashion he shouts orders to them.

If they win Hegemont promised them gold and fine wine -

once assembled at the hillside they begin the steep climb.

Cautiously, Allerdale watches for clues

which would signal that Hegemont is about to debut.

Then a snap of a twig sounds, and the order is given,

"No quarter, no prisoners!  Just be sure that we win!"

Each in the Red army says a quick silent prayer,

in hope of surviving this day's massacre.

Others shed a tear for the many that will die,

then the fighting begins with a thousand battle cries.

Oh, Quadrinall with trees so tall,

so undisturbed from spring till fall.

When morning comes and dawn's light buds,

>           your fertile soil will be soaked with blood.

(III)
The Red archers fire with so deadly an aim

that hundreds of Black troops lay dead or maimed.

Then Hegemont sends horsemen into the attack,

and in seconds most archers lie dead on their back.


Next, some Red foot soldiers stalk the left flank,

while Allerdale's knights attack the right ranks.

But, Hegemont expected this sort of sly game,

and soon the remaining Red archers were slain.


For hours the battle remained a stalemate,

with both sides reduced to a sad and sorry state.

By twilight King Allerdale was close to defeat,

yet his valiant men fought on and would not retreat.


With confidence, Hegemont felt victory was near,

but carelessly forgot to protect his rear.

Now Allerdale noticed this one fatal mistake,

then orders his knights to attack without haste.

Toward the back of the battle Red knights start to ride,

and with sudden aghast Hegemont views his rear side.

He desperately tries to regroup all his men,

but the effort fell vain and he could not defend.

This only confused and scattered his force,

and within a few minutes the battle was lost.

Now proud Hegemont could not accept this defeat,

and bolted on horseback toward Allerdale's seat.

With rage in his heart and his sword in his hand

Hegemont's single-most thought was one final stand.

Then Allerdale turned and saw his opponent's sword rise,

and he cut through the throat of the one he despised.

Oh, Quadrinall with trees so tall,

so undisturbed from spring till fall.

When morning comes and dawn's light buds,

your fertile soil will be soaked with blood.

Upon your green hilltop lay thousands of dead;

by midday the funeral tears will have been shed.

For their sorrow the Red forces have but one consolation:

their countrymen's deaths brought life back to their nation.

*TERMINAT HORA DIEM; TERMINAT AUCTOR OPUS*

# ABOUT THE AUTHOR

Frank S. Farello was born and raised in New York -
and together with his Wife and family,
continues to do so.

Made in United States
North Haven, CT
31 May 2025

69378890R00128